SMILES

SMILES
a photographic celebration

If you don't start the day with a smile,

it's not too late to start practicing

for tomorrow…

Anonymous

A smile is a light in the window of the soul

indicating that the heart is at home.

Unknown

7

Happiness is a perfume you cannot

pour on others without getting a

few drops on yourself.

Ralph Waldo Emerson

Smiling is contagious; you catch it like the flu,

When someone smiled at me today, I started smiling too.

I passed around the corner, and someone saw my grin—

When he smiled I realized, I'd passed it on to him.

Anonymous

A winning smile makes

winners of us all.

Anonymous

Smile—

it's the second best thing

you can do with your lips.

Unknown

A laugh is a smile that bursts.

Mary H. Waldrip

People don't notice

whether it's summer

or winter when

they're happy.

Anton Chekhov

The most

wasted day is

that on which

one has not

laughed.

Nicholas Chamfort

21

A smile

is a passport

that will take you

anywhere you want to go.

Anonymous

A really happy person is

one who can enjoy the scenery

when on a detour.

Unknown

Laugh

and the world

laughs with you.

Ellen Wheeler Wilcox

27

A smile happens in a flash,

but its memory can last a lifetime.

Anonymous

Mirth is like a flash of lightning

that breaks through a gloom

of clouds, and glitters for a

moment: cheerfulness keeps up

a kind of daylight in the mind.

Joseph Addison

The little things are most worthwhile—a quiet

word, a look, a smile.

Margaret Lindsey

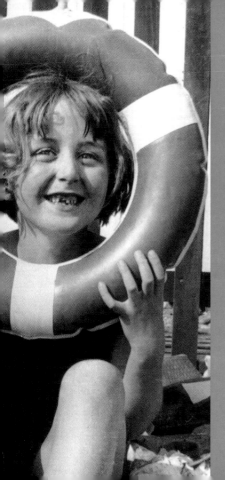

Happiness isn't

something you

experience; it's

something you

remember.

Oscar Levent

35

The world always looks brighter from behind a smile.

Anonymous

If you feel a smile begin,

don't leave it undetected—

let's start an epidemic quick,

and get the world infected.

Anonymous

There is no duty we so much underrate

as the duty of being happy.

Robert Louis Stevenson

The best way to cheer yourself

is to try to cheer someone else up.

Mark Twain

Smile, it's free therapy.

Doug Horton

Everything is funny

as long as it is happening

to someone else.

Will Rogers

47

Laughter is the best medicine.

Proverb

Do not take life seriously.

You will never get out of it alive.

Elbert Hubbard

No matter how grouchy you're feeling,

You'll find the smile more or less healing.

It grows in a wreath

All around the front teeth—

Thus preserving the face from congealing.

Anthony Euwer

The world is like a mirror, you see?

Smile, and your friends smile back.

Zen saying

Happiness depends,

as nature shows,

Less on exterior things

than most suppose.

William Cowper

We smile because we are happy.

But we also become happy because we smile.

Unknown

It is in the enjoyment

and not in the mere

possession that makes

for happiness.

Michel de Montaigne

Most smiles

are started by

other smiles.

Smile first.

Unknown

A smile shared is a smile doubled.

Anonymous

Why not seize the pleasure at once?

How often is happiness destroyed

by preparation, foolish preparation!

Jane Austen

It's almost impossible to smile on the outside

without feeling better on the inside.

Anonymous

It takes seventy-two muscles to frown,

but only thirteen to smile.

Anonymous

If in doubt, smile.

Anonymous

…All that we need to make us really happy

is something to be enthusiastic about.

Charles Kingsley

If you would like to spoil the day for

a grouch, give him a smile.

Anonymous

A smile is a

powerful weapon;

you can even

break ice with it.

Anonymous

Happiness is no laughing matter.

Richard Whately

Laugh and grow strong.

St. Ignatius of Loyola

If you have only one smile in you,

give it to the people you love.

Maya Angelou

Danger and delight

grow on one stalk.

English Proverb

Humor is the great thing, the saving thing. The minute it crops up, all our irritations and resentments slip away, and a sunny spirit takes their place.

Mark Twain

I hear a smile.

Richard Assheton

If you're going to be able to look back

on something and laugh about it, you

might as well laugh about it now.

Marie Osmond

The secret of happiness is to

admire without desiring.

F. H. Bradley

I thought about that smile,

then I realized its worth,

A single smile, just like mine,

could travel round the earth.

Anonymous

Of all the things we wear,

a smile and a good humor

are the most important.

Unknown

Life may be short, but a smile takes but a second.

Arab saying

Find expression for a joy,

and you will intensify its ecstasy.

Unknown

Never frown because you never know who

might be falling in love with your smile.

Justine Milton

The smile that you send out returns to you.

Indian Proverb

A smile costs nothing,

but gives much.

Anonymous

Picture Credits

All images Hulton Getty Picture Collection.

cover: A young girl smiles through a rubber ring on Brighton beach, 1934

page 5: Baby smiling, 1942.

page 6: Two young women enjoy tubs of ice-cream, 1937.

page 9: Two flappers on a beach with a fishing rod and their catch, circa 1928.

page 10: Two youngsters riding on a bicycle: a potentially dangerous stunt that is also illegal, circa 1955.

page 13: Actor Jose Ferrer hears the news that he has won an Academy Award for his performance in "Cyrano de Bergerac."

page 14: A couple laughing at London's Lyceum dance hall, 1951.

page 17: Michelle Durlow, bouncing on a hopper, 1971.

page 19: Prima ballerina Margot Fonteyn feeding a pigeon in Milan, 1957.

page 20: Three women wearing identical straw hats and enjoying themselves on a ride at the fair, 1951.

page 22: Alan Bartlett Shepard, the astronaut and first American in space, wears his space suit and a smile during training for the Apollo 14 mission, 1970. © NASA/Hulton Archive

page 25: Horse racing commentator Joanne Mathews takes a break from the horse, 1956.

page 26: Jazz musicians Benny Goodman, Ziggy Elman, and Vernon Brown laughing, circa 1945.

page 28: A courting couple share a joke, circa 1955.

page 31: Racegoers manage a smile despite the rain showers, 1931.

page 33: A woman perches on a mooring post to play a guitar on the River Thames, 1931.

page 34: Two young girls smile through rubber rings on Brighton beach, 1934.

page 37: An elderly couple standing outside the door of their condemned house, 1954.

page 39: A young girl wearing goggles and fins in the bath, circa 1955.

page 41: Sherree Danton, Pat Lawrence, and Wendy Graham enjoying the wind machine at the opening of a festival fun fair, 1957.

page 42: Polish tobacco farmers in Connecticut, 1940.

page 45: A house servant enjoys a laugh in the garden, circa 1890.

page 46: Girls from Plymouth, Massachusetts, enjoying the snow with a hovel race, circa 1950.

page 49: Two bathing beauties enjoy a joke with a vertriloquist's dummy, circa 1956.

page 51: Mr Ron Brewer runs a home for unwanted donkeys, with "Betty", a young foal donkey, 1964.

page 52: A cheerful group of soccer fans, 1952.

page 55: Children at school in post-war Dusseldorf, 1946.

page 56: Jenny Dve with her Afghan hounds, 1980.

page 59: A smiling boy, surrounded by jars of candy, 1949.

page 60: Actress Rosemary Lane clings to a plastic lilo whilst swimming in Lake Arrowhead with actor Jeffrey Lynn, in a scene from the film "Family Reunion," 1939.

page 63: Two ladies play whilst in the park, 1942.

page 65: Two waitresses take a break to share a laugh in the kitchen of Berns Restaurant, 1956.

page 66: Marilyn Monroe frolicking on the beach near her Hollywood home during a break from filming, circa 1955.

page 69: a group of children enjoying a Punch and Judy show, circa 1950.

page 70: A young Brownie Girl Guide holding a duckling whilst another is standing on her head, 1939.

page 73: Raquel Torres and Josephine Dunn, standing on a hydroplane, circa 1934.

page 74: Young farmer holds the school's "farm" geese, from their own pig and poultry farm, 1940.

page 77: Helen Twelvetrees, circa 1936.

page 78: A girl and boy smile at each other while eating ice cream at a soda fountain corner, circa 1955. © Lambert/Hulton Archive.

page 81: Michael Wilding shares a laugh with French co-star Odile Versois during the filming of "Into the Blue", 1950.

page 83: Four members of the American Red Cross stationed in England: Eleanor Stevenson, Patricia Hartnett, Adelaide Johnson, and Eileen Tyler, circa 1945.

page 84: Jazz bandleader Tommy Dorsey and his wife, Pat, smile at each other, circa 1945.

page 87: Two women enjoying a fun fair ride, 1952.

page 89: "Uncle Arthur" in charge of a laughing competition for children at a carnival day, 1954.

page 90: A young man and woman smile as they run through the snow, circa 1945. © Lambert/Hulton Archive.

page 93: A policeman displays a prize-winning vegetable which he grew in his back garden, 1938.

page 94: Six-year-old Martin Stephens cuddles up to a giant teddy bear, 1956.

page 96: Louis "Satchmo" ("Satchelmouth") Armstrong, the great jazz trumpeter and vocalist, relaxes and has a laugh, 1968.

page 99: Three women modelling fashionable swimwear and large straw hats, 1947.

page 100: A young boy having fun on a shute, 1953.

page 103: A girl and boy smile while jumping in the air during a potato sack race, circa 1945. © Lambert/Hulton Archive.

page 104: A couple laugh as they enjoy a dance at a night club, in Harlem, New York, circa 1939.

page 107: A young couple out boating together, 1956.

page 108: A man holds his granddaughter, 1945.

Published by MQ Publications Limited
12 The Ivories, 6–8 Northampton Street, London, N1 2HY
Tel: 020 7359 2244 / Fax: 020 7359 1616
e-mail: mail@ mqpublications.com

Copyright © MQ Publications Limited, 2002

ISBN: 1-84072-170-7

3 5 7 9 0 8 6 4

Cover design: John Casey
Design: Philippa Jarvis
Series Editor: Elizabeth Carr

Printed and bound in China